What Theosophy Does for Us

By C. W. Leadbeater

Copyright © 2021 Lamp of Trismegistus. All rights reserved. No part of this publication may be reproduced or transmitted in any form or by any means, electronic or mechanical, including photocopying, recording, or by any information storage and retrieval system, without permission in writing from Lamp of Trismegistus. Reviewers may quote brief passages.

ISBN: 978-1-63118-574-8

Esoteric Classics

Other Books in this Series and Related Titles

Aurora of the Philosophers by Paracelsus (978-1-63118-507-6)

Clairvoyance and Psychic Abilities by A Besant &c (978-1-63118-403-1)

The Feminine Occult by various authors (978-1-63118-711-7)

Rosicrucian Rules, Secret Signs, Codes and Symbols by various (978-1-63118-488-8)

An Outline of Theosophy by C W Leadbeater (978-1-63118-452-9)

Paracelsus, the Four Elements and Their Spirits by M P Hall (978-1-63118-400-0)

Essays on Ancient Magic by Helena P Blavatsky (978-1-63118-535-9)

Essays on the Esoteric Tradition of Karma by A Besant &c (978-1-63118-426-0)

The Use of Evil by Annie Besant (978-1-63118-532-8)

The Alchemical Catechism of Paracelsus by Paracelsus (978-1-63118-513-7)

Alchemy in the Nineteenth Century by Helena P Blavatsky (978-1-63118-446-8)

Qabbalistic Teachings and the Tree of Life by M P Hall (978-1-63118-482-6)

The Historic, Mythic and Mystic Christ by Annie Besant (978–1–63118–533–5)

The Hidden Mysteries of Christianity by Annie Besant (978–1–63118–534–2)

History, Analysis and Secret Tradition of the Tarot by Hall &c (978-1-63118-445-1)

Crystal Vision Through Crystal Gazing by Frater Achad (978-1-63118-455-0)

The Golden Verses of Pythagoras: Five Translations (978-1-63118-479-6)

Arcane Formulas or Mental Alchemy by W W Atkinson (978-1-63118-459-8)

The Machinery of the Mind by Dion Fortune (978-1-63118-451-2)

The A E Waite Reader: A Selection of Occult Essays (978-1-63118-515-1)

The Leadbeater Reader: A Selection of Occult Essays (978-1-63118-483-3)

Audio versions are also available on Audible, Amazon and Apple

Other Books in this Series and Related Titles

Spiritual Life for Man by Annie Besant (978–1–63118–573–1)

The Mysteries by Annie Besant (978–1–63118–572–4)

Fundamental Ideas of Theosophy by Bhagwan Das (978–1–63118–571–7)

Dreams: What They Are and Caused by C W Leadbeater (978–1–63118–570–0)

Communication Between Different Worlds by Annie Besant (978–1–63118–569–4)

Animism, Magic and the Omnipotence of Thought by S Freud (978–1–63118–568–7)

Buddhism by F Otto Schrader (978–1–63118–567–0)

Death by W W Westcott (978–1–63118–566–3)

The Religion of Theosophy by Bhagwan Das (978–1–63118–565–6)

The Spirit of Zoroastrianism by Henry S Olcott (978–1–63118–564–9)

The Brotherhood of Religions by Annie Besant (978–1–63118–563–2)

Fourth Book of Maccabees by Josephus (978-1-63118-562-5)

The Story of Ahikar by Ahiqar (978-1-63118-561-8)

Vision of the Spirit by C. Jinarajadasa (978-1-63118-560-1)

Occult Arts by William Q. Judge (978-1-63118-559-5)

Kali the Mother by Sister Nivedita (978-1-63118-558-8)

Love and Death by Sri Aurobindo (978–1–63118–557–1)

Times and Seasons Volume 1, Numbers 4-6 (978-1-63118-556-4)

The Book of John Whitmer by John Whitmer (978-1-63118-554-0)

Interesting Account of Several Remarkable Visions (978-1-63118-553-3)

Private Diary of Joseph Smith 1832-1834 (978-1-63118-546-5)

Audio versions are also available on Audible, Amazon and Apple

Table of Contents

Introduction...7

What Theosophy Does for Us...9

The Work of the Theosophists...35

INTRODUCTION

The word "esoteric" can be difficult to define. Esotericism in general can be seen less as a system of beliefs and more as a category, which encompasses numerous, different systems of beliefs. It's a bit of juxtaposition, since the word "esoteric" indicates something that few people know about, while the term itself broadly covers numerous philosophies, practices, areas of study and belief systems.

In a greater sense, Esotericism acts as a storehouse for secret knowledge, which is often considered ancient (by *tradition, if not by fact)*, passed down from generation to generation, in private. At various times in history, simply possessing the knowledge of some of these subjects, was considered illegal and a jailable offence, if discovered. This usually included such general topics as Alchemy, Pharmacology, Qabalah, Hermeticism, Occultism, Ceremonial Magic, Astrology, Divination, Rosicrucianism and so on. Collectively, these areas of study were often referred to as the esoteric sciences.

Sometimes, the outer garment of a subject isn't esoteric, while what is hidden beneath it, is. As an example, Freemasonry isn't necessarily esoteric by nature (at *least not anymore)*, but certain signs, passwords and handshakes given to the candidate during their initiation, are in fact, esoteric, in the sense that they are hidden from the general public.

Today, in the twenty-first century, such topics are readily available at bookstores across the country, and numerous mainsteam publishers offer beginners guides and coffee-table volumes on many of these subjects, intended for mass appeal. Books like *"The Secret"* have turned previously arcane topics into household knowledge. All that being the case, however, it isn't to say that there still aren't buried secrets to uncover, ancient wisdom being ignored and forgotten mysteries to be explored. In fact, it is often that we are only able to further our own studies by standing on the shoulders of these disappearing giants.

Lamp of Trismegistus is doing its part to help preserve humanity's esoteric history by making some of these classics available to those students who are seeking to unearth the knowledge of these ancient colossi.

So, be sure to check other titles from our *Esoteric Classics* series, as well as our *Occult Fiction, Theosophical Classics, Foundations of Freemasonry Series, Supernatural Fiction, Paranormal Research Series, Studies in Buddhism* and our *Christian Apocrypha Series.* You can also download the audio versions of most of these titles from Amazon, Apple or Audible, for learning on the go.

WHAT THEOSOPHY DOES FOR US

There are certain great basic facts of life about which every thinking man desires accurate information — such facts as the existence and nature of God and His relation to man; we desire to know whence we came and whither we are going and what is the object of our existence. There are in the world many forms of religion, and each of these forms has propounded its own theories with regard to these matters, but these theories have differed widely, and each has bitterly assailed and ridiculed the beliefs of the others, so that the majority of men have come to think that upon all these points there is no certain information available.

So it comes to them as a surprise to find that there is a coherent and reasonable theory of the universe — a plain declaration of the great facts of nature, so far as they are known — a statement which is not to be accepted as a creed, but to be studied and investigated. Theosophy is such a statement — a definite science the result of many centuries of research and experiment, yet verified in our day by many of its students, and verifiable by anyone who is willing to take the trouble to qualify himself for such enquiry.

Theosophy is not a religion, but it bears to the religions the same relation as did the ancient philosophies; it does not contradict any of them, but it explains and harmonises them all. It teaches that truth on all those important points of which we have spoken is attainable, and that there is a great body of knowledge about them already existing. It considers all the various religions as statements of that truth from different points of view, and for evidence of this it points to the fact that however much these faiths may seem to differ, its teachings explain them all. It shows us also the relation between religion and science - that they are not hostile to one another, as is usually supposed, but that, on the contrary, true religion should welcome science, as affording the means of proof for its teachings, while science may learn from religion the direction in which it may most usefully push its investigations. Theosophy is itself a science, and the greatest of all, for it is the Science of the Soul; it carries scientific methods into higher realms and applies them to the consideration of a vast field of facts which lie beyond the reach of the physical senses. It solves for us many of the most difficult problems of life, and explains for us many mysteries, bringing them all together as parts of a connected scheme, and thus making them at once intelligible and rational.

From the investigations that have been made, there emerge three great basic truths, not metaphysical speculations, not pious opinions, but definite scientific facts. proved and examined over and over again by many students. These truths are:

1. God exists, and He is good. He is the great life-giver who dwells within us and without us, and is undying and eternally beneficent. He is not heard, nor seen, nor touched, yet is perceived by the man who desires perception.

2. Man is immortal, and his future is one whose glory and splendour have no limit.

3. A Divine law of absolute justice rules the world, so that each man is in truth his own judge, the dispenser of glory or gloom to himself, the decreer of his life, his reward, his punishment.

Since the object of this paper is not to explain the scheme, but to describe its results in daily life, I may refer the reader, for further exposition of it, to *An Outline of Theosophy*.

When those three great basic truths and all the deductions which naturally follow from them are thoroughly comprehended, they introduce so radical a change into man's life that it is not easy within reasonable compass to give any idea of its extent. The best that can be done is to mention a few leading ideas, leaving the reader to follow out the necessary ramifications for himself.

Finding that there is a Supreme Power which is directing the course of evolution and that He is all-wise and all-loving, we see that everything which exists within His scheme must be intended to further its progress. We realise that all things are working together for good, not only in the far distant future, but also now and here. The final attainment of unspeakable glory is an absolute certainty for every son of man, whatever may be his present condition. But that is by no means all; here and at this present moment he is on his way towards that glory; and all the circumstances surrounding him are intended to help and not to hinder him, if only they are rightly understood. It is sadly true that in the world there is much of evil and of sorrow and of suffering; yet, from the higher point of view we may see that, terrible though this be, it is only temporary and superficial, and is all being utilised as a factor in the progress.

While we look at it from its own level it is almost impossible to see this, but if we will raise ourselves above it and look upon it with, the eyes of the spirit we shall regard it as a whole, and thus we shall comprehend it. While we are looking from beneath at the underside of life, with our eyes fixed all the time upon some apparent evil, we can never gain a true grasp of its meaning; but if we rise above it to the higher planes of thought and of consciousness we can look down and understand it in its entirety. So we can see that in very truth all is well. Not only that all will be well in some remote future, but that even now in this moment in the midst of incessant strife and apparent evil, the mighty current of evolution is still flowing, and so all is well because all is moving on in perfect order towards the final goal.

Regard the roaring rapids of some rolling river, such as Niagara, and picture to yourself some tiny insect being swept down upon the surface of the water. Think how that water boils and foams, and surges and rushes this way and that as it dashes among the rugged rocks, and realise how impossible it would be for that tiny insect to see anything beyond the strife and the stress and the foam and the beating backwards and forwards; how to him, inevitably, that must seem the whole world, nothing but a confusion and a struggle and a buffeting, carrying him sometimes in one direction and sometimes in the other, without any ordered progress or any comprehensible object. Yet we have only to rise above all that confusion, to stand upon the bank and look down upon it, and we observe that the whole body of water is moving steadily onwards, and that though, here and there, there are little eddies in which part of it, for the time, seems to be running backwards, in reality the very eddies themselves are all the time sweeping forwards with the rest.

Just so the philosopher who can raise his consciousness above the storm and stress of worldly life looking down upon it from above recognises what seems to us to be evil and notes how it is apparently pressing backward against the great stream of progress; but he also sees that the onward sweep of the Divine law of evolution bears the same relation to this superficial evil as does the tremendous torrent of Niagara to the fleckings of foam upon its surface. So while he sympathises deeply with all who suffer, he yet realises what will be the end of that suffering; and so for him despair or hopelessness is impossible. He applies this consideration to his own sorrows and troubles as well as to those of the world, and therefore one great result of his Theosophy is a perfect serenity — even more than that, a perpetual cheerfulness and joy.

For him there is an utter absence of worry, because in truth there is nothing left to worry about, since he knows that all must be well. His higher science makes him a confirmed optimist, for it shows him that, whatever of evil there may be in any person or in any movement, it is of necessity temporary because it is opposed to the resistless stream of evolution; whereas, whatever is good in any person or any movement must necessarily be persistent and useful because it has behind it the omnipotence of that current, and therefore it must abide and it must prevail. Yet it must not for a moment be supposed that, because he is so fully assured of the final triumph of good, he remains careless of or unmoved by the evils which exist in the world around him. He knows that it is his duty to combat these to the utmost of his power because in doing this he is working upon the side of the great evolutionary force and is bringing nearer the time of its ultimate victory. None will be more active than he in labouring for the good, even though he is absolutely free from the feeling of helplessness and hopelessness which so often oppresses those who are striving to help their fellow-men.

Another most valuable result of Theosophical study is the absence of fear. Many people are constantly anxious or worried about something or other; they are fearing lest this or that should happen to them; lest this or that combination may fail, and so all the while they are in a condition of unrest. The major part of their fear is wholly unnecessary, and most of the things feared never come to pass; but nevertheless the fact remains that large numbers of people are constantly giving themselves a great deal of unnecessary suffering in this way. Most serious of all for many is the fear of death. Quite a large number of people seem to have it always in their minds as an ever-haunting dread — a sword of Damocles ever hanging over their heads, ready to fall upon them at any moment.

The whole of that feeling is entirely swept away for the man who understands the Theosophical teaching. When we realise the great truth of reincarnation, when we know that we have often before laid aside physical bodies, then we shall see that death is no more to us than sleep; that just as sleep comes in between our days of work and gives us rest and refreshment, so between these days of labour here on earth which we call lives, there comes the long night of astral and of heavenly life to give us rest and refreshment and to help us on our way. To the Theosophist death is simply the laying aside for a time of this robe of flesh. He knows that it is his duty to preserve that bodily vesture as long as he can, to gain all the experience he can; but when the time comes for him to lay it down, he will do so thankfully, because he knows that the next stage will be a very much pleasanter one than this. Thus he will have no fear of death, although he realizes that he must live his life to the appointed end, because he is here for the purpose of progress, and that progress is the one truly momentous matter. See what a difference that makes in a man's conception of life; the object is not to earn so much money, not to obtain such and such a position; the one important thing, when we really comprehend it, is to carry out the Divine plan. For this we are here, and everything else should give way to it. It needs only that we shall understand the facts, and all fear at once ceases.

Another great point which we gain from our Theosophical teaching is that we have no longer any religious fears or worries or troubles. Many of our noblest and best people are constantly morbidly introspective, constantly fearing whether at the last they may not somehow be cast away; whether they may not fall short in some way, they scarcely understand how, of the demands which their faith makes upon them.

All that is swept aside when we see clearly that progress towards the highest is the Divine Will for us; that we cannot escape from that progress; that whatever comes in our way and whatever happens to us is meant to help us along that line; that we ourselves are absolutely the only people that can delay our advance. When we really know this, what a difference it makes in the aspect of life! No longer do we trouble and fear about ourselves; we simply go on and do the duty which comes nearest, in the best way that we can, confident that if we do this, all will be well for us without our perpetually worrying.

True, we are told in the wise Greek proverb: *Know thyself*. True, it is our business to know ourselves, and to discover our own weak points; but that also must be done according to reason and according to common-sense, and we must not be like those tiny children who, when they make a garden, are constantly pulling up their plants to see how much they are growing. That is exactly what so many good people are always doing — they are perpetually pulling themselves up by the roots to see how they are getting on, instead of being satisfied quietly to do their duty, and trying to help their fellows in the race, knowing that the great Divine Power behind will press them onward slowly and steadily and do for them all that can be done, so long as their faces are set steadfastly in the right direction, so long as they do all that they reasonably can.

Since we are thus all part of one great evolution and all very literally the children of one Father, we see that the Universal Brotherhood of Humanity is no mere poetical conception, but a definite fact; not a dream of something which is to be in the dim distance of Utopia, but a condition existing here and now; and that is why the promotion, the realisation of that Universal Brotherhood is the first object of the Theosophical Society. And the certainty of this all-embracing fraternity gives us a wider outlook upon life and a broad impersonal point of view from which to regard everything. The ordinary man looks at everything from a personal point of view; the first thing and often the only thing that he thinks about is how a certain occurrence is going to affect him; if he thinks of its effect on the community at large it is only as an after-thought. Theosophy teaches us that the real interests of all are in truth identical, and that no man can ever make a real gain for himself at the cost of loss or suffering to someone else. Once more we must insist that this also is not taught as a pious belief, but is proved as a scientific fact.

Many a man is under the delusion that he gains much for himself when he cheats or injures another; he may even think that he can prove it by showing the shillings and pence which he has amassed in this nefarious manner. But in truth that man is taking a ludicrously partial view of the case and is leaving out of account absolutely every factor which is of any permanent value. For there is something higher and greater in a man than the physical body, which is after all nothing but a vesture, and that which is of importance is not the effect of any given transaction upon the vesture, but upon the man who wears it; and it is found by investigation that the effect of any such fraudulent action upon the true man, the soul, is limiting and debasing to the last degree; so that through his ignorance of the facts, such a man is seriously hindering his own progress for the sake of a very small apparent acquisition.

Since humanity is literally a whole, nothing which injures one man can ever be really for the good of any other, for the harm done influences not only the doer but all those who are about him. So the student soon comes to know that there is no such thing as a private gain at another man's cost and that the only true advantage for him is that benefit which he shares with all. He sees also that any advance which he makes in the way of spiritual progress or development is something secured not for himself alone but for others, as we shall see later when we come to write on the subject of thepower of thought.

If he gains knowledge and self-control he assuredly acquires much for himself, yet he takes nothing away from anyone else, but on the contrary he helps and strengthens others. Cognisant as he is of the absolute spiritual unity of humanity, he knows that in this lower world also, in real truth, the interest of one can never be opposed to the interest of all, so that no true profit can be made by one man which is not made in the name and for the sake of all humanity; that one man's progress must be a lifting of the burden of all the others; that one man's advance in spiritual things means a very slight yet not imperceptible advance to humanity as a whole; and that everyone who bears sorrow and suffering nobly in his struggle towards the light; is lifting a little of the heavy load of the sorrow and suffering of his brothers as well.

When he recognises this brotherhood, not merely as a hope cherished by despairing men, but as a definite fact following in scientific series from all other facts, when he sees this as an absolute certainty, his attitude towards all those around him naturally changes very greatly. It becomes a posture ever of helpfulness, ever of the deepest sympathy, for he sees that nothing which clashes with their higher interest can ever be the right thing for him to do or can ever be good for him in any way. And so it naturally follows that he becomes filled with the widest possible tolerance and charity. He cannot but be always tolerant, because his philosophy shows him that it matters little what a man believes so long as he is a good man and true. Charitable also he must be, because his wider knowledge enables him to make allowance for many things which the ordinary man does not understand. The standard of the Theosophical student as to right and wrong is always higher than that of the less-instructed man; yet he is far gentler than the latter in his feeling towards the sinner, because he comprehends more of human nature. He realises how the sin appeared to the sinner at the moment of its commission, and so he makes more allowance than could possibly be made by the man who is ignorant of all this.

He goes further than tolerance, charity, sympathy; he feels positive love towards mankind, and that leads him to adopt a position of ever-watchful helpfulness. The child who deeply loves his mother is always watching for an opportunity of doing some little thing for her, something that he knows will please her or save her trouble. It is just that attitude of watching for an opportunity to help which the Theosophist adopts towards his fellows. He feels that every contact with others is for him an opportunity, and Theosophy brings him so much additional knowledge, that there is hardly any case in which it does not enable him to give advice or help.

Not that he is perpetually thrusting his opinions upon other people; on the contrary he observes that just this is one of the commonest of mistakes made by the uninstructed. If the ordinary man has a definite opinion of his own, whether it be upon matters religious, political, or social, or upon any of the other subjects of common discussion, he is for ever endeavouring to force that opinion upon others and to make them think exactly as he does. The Theosophist knows that all this is a very foolish waste of energy, and therefore he declines to argue. If anyone desires from him explanation or advice he is more than willing to give it; yet he has no sort of wish to convert anyone else to his own way of thinking.

In every relation of life this idea of helpfulness comes into play — not only with regard to our fellow-men, but also with regard to the vast animal kingdom which surounds us. Units of this kingdom are often brought into very close relation with us, and this is for us an opportunity of doing something for them. We must remember that these animals also are our brothers, even though they may be younger brothers. It is the same great Divine Life which animates, them, even though it be a later wave, a less developed outpouring of that life. Still, they are our brothers, and we owe a fraternal duty to them also — so to act and so to think that our relation with them shall be always for their good and never for their harm.

Pre-eminently and above all else, Theosophy is a doctrine of common-sense. It puts before us, so far as we can know them, the facts about God and man and the relation between them; and then it instructs us to take these facts into account, and act in relation to them with ordinary reason and common-sense. This is all that it asks from any man as regards life. It suggests to him to regulate his life according to these laws of evolution which it has taught him. That is all, yet it means a great deal; for it gives the man a totally different standpoint, and a touchstone by which to try everything — his own thoughts and feelings, and his own actions first of all, and then those things which come before him in the world outside himself.

Always he applies this criterion, is the thing right or wrong ? Does it help evolution or does it hinder it ? If a thought or a feeling arises within himself, he may see at once by this test whether it is one that he ought to encourage. If it is for the greatest good of the greatest number, then all is well; if it may hinder or cause harm to any being in its progress, then it is evil and to be avoided. Exactly the same reasoning holds good if he is called upon to decide with regard to anything outside of himself. If from that point of view the thing be a good thing, then he can conscientiously support it; if not, then it is not for him.

For the man who sees the truth in this way the question of personal interest does not come into the case at all, and he thinks simply of the good of evolution as a whole. This gives the man a definite foothold, a clear criterion, and removes from him the pain of indecision and hesitation. The Will of God is man's evolution; whatever therefore helps on that evolution must be good, whatever stands in the way of it and delays it, that thing must be wrong, even though it may have on its side all the weight of public opinion and of immemorial tradition. It is true that all about us we see infringements of the Divine Law taking place, yet we know that the law is far stronger than the petty wills of those who ignorantly disobey it; we know that in working along with the law we are certainly working for the future, and that, though at the passing moment our efforts may not be appreciated, the future will assuredly do us justice. Therefore we care little for the judgment of those who do not yet understand, since our knowledge of the governing laws enables us to work in the right direction.

Of no less importance are the practical deductions which flow from the second of the great truths which we stated at the beginning of this paper; for to understand that the true man is the soul and not the body means an absolute revolution from the concepts of the majority of men around us. Our common expressions in every-day life show the most astounding practical materialism, for we constantly speak of *my soul* showing that we ordinarily regard the body as the self and the supposed soul as part of its property. Until we have entirely rid ourselves of this extraordinary delusion that the body is the man, it is quite impossible that we should at all appreciate the real facts of the case. A little investigation soon shows us that the body is only a vehicle by means of which the man manifests himself in connection with this particular type of gross matter out of which our visible world is built, and that the man himself has an existence quite apart from his body, capable of being carried on at a distance from it when it is living and entirely without it when , it is dead.

This being so, it becomes evident at once that it is the life of the soul only which is really of moment, and that everything connected with the body must unhesitatingly be subordinated to those higher interests. The student knows that this earth-life is given to him for the purpose of progress and that that progress is the one really important thing. We shall readily see what a difference this makes in his conception of life; the objects which men ordinarily put before themselves at once fade into the background, for he sees that whether he earns a certain amount of money or whether he obtains some particular position is a matter of comparatively little moment. The one vital thing, now that he understands life, is to carry out the Divine Plan, since it is for that reason that he is here, and everything else must give way to that. The real purpose of his life is the unfoldment of his powers as a soul, the development of his character. It is with this object only that he descends into physical life, in order that through the physical body he may gain experience which would not be possible to him on a higher plane, and may thus develop within himself permanent qualities.

Closer study will show him that he possesses other vehicles besides the physical body, and that through all of these he has lessons to learn; so that there must be development not only of the physical body, but also of the emotional nature, of the mind, and of the spiritual perceptions. The detailed method by which all this can be done will be found in our Theosophical literature; but half of the battle is already won when the man has realized the necessity for this effort and is determined to make it. In connection with this he discovers three great points:

1. That nothing short of absolute perfection is expected of him in regard to this development. 2. That all power with regard to it is in his own hands.

3. That he has all eternity before him in which to attain this perfection, but that the sooner it is gained, the happier and more useful will he be.

He sees that what he has been in the habit of calling his life is nothing but a day at school, and that his physical body is merely a temporary vesture assumed for the purpose of learning through it. He knows at once that this purpose of learning the lesson is the only one of any real importance, and that the man who allows himself to be diverted from that purpose by any consideration whatever is acting with inconceivable stupidity. To him who thus grasps the truth, the life of the ordinary person devoted exclusively to physical objects, to the acquisition of wealth or fame, appears the merest child's play — a senseless sacrifice of all that is really worth having, for the sake of a few moments' gratification of the lower part of man's nature. The student "sets his affections on things above and not on things on the earth", not only because he sees this to be the right course of action, but because he realizes very clearly the valuelessness of these things of earth. He always tries to take the higher point of view, for he knows that the lower is utterly unreliable — that the lower desires and feelings gather round him like a dense fog and make it impossible for him to see anything clearly from that level. Whenever he finds a struggle going on within him — the "law of the members warring against the law of the mind as St. Paul puts it — he remembers that he himself is the higher, and that this, which is the lower, is not the real self, but merely an uncontrolled part of one of its vehicles. He identifies himself never with the lower, but always with the higher; he stands on its side, because he knows that the soul is the true man.

The great law of evolution is steadily pressing us on, sweeping us ever onward and upward along the course that all must take sooner or later. But it is obvious that the better we understand the Divine Law under which we are living, the easier and the more rapid will be our progress. No doubt even with the very best intentions and efforts we shall make many mistakes and shall often fall by the way; but we need not for this reason become the victims of despair. Although we may fail a thousand times on the way towards our goal, our reason for trying to reach it remains just as strong after the thousandth fall as it was at the beginning, so that it would not only be useless but very unwise and very wrong to give way to despondency and hopelessness. The work has to be done, the goal has to be attained, and each man must always start from where he individually stands: it is futile for him to think that he will wait until he reaches some other position. Therefore, however often he may fail, he must still get up and go on again, for the road of progress has to be trodden.

The sooner we begin it the better for us; not only because it is far easier for us now than it will be if we leave the effort until later, but chiefly because, if we make the endeavour now and succeed in achieving some progress, if we rise thereby to some higher level, we are in a position to hold out a helping hand to those who have not reached even that step of the ladder which we have gained. In this way we may take a part, however humble it may be, in the great Divine work of evolution, every one of us, because each has his own position and his own opportunities. No matter how low his present status may be, yet there is someone still lower to whom he can hold out a helping hand, to whom he can be useful. The Theosophical teaching shows him that he has arrived at his present position only by a very slow process of growth, and so he cannot expect instantaneous attainment of perfection; but it also shows him how inevitable is the great law of cause and effect, and he sees that when he once grasps the working of that law he can use it intelligently in regard to mental and moral development, just as on the physical plane we can employ for our own assistance those laws of nature the working of which, we have learned to understand.

One of the most important practical results of a thorough comprehension of Theosophical truth is the entire change which it necessarily brings about in our attitude towards death. It is impossible to calculate the vast amount of utterly unnecessary sorrow and misery which mankind in the aggregate has suffered simply from its ignorance with regard to this one matter of death. There is among us a mass of false and foolish belief along this line which has worked untold evil in the past and is causing indescribable affliction in the present, and its complete eradication would be one of the greatest benefits that could be conferred upon the human race. This benefit Theosophy at once bestows upon those who, from their study of philosophy in past lives, find themselves able to accept it. It robs death forthwith of all its terror and much of its sorrow, and enables us to see it in its true proportions and to understand its place in the scheme of our evolution.

The man who understands what death is knows that there can be no need to fear it or to mourn over it, whether it comes to himself or to those whom he loves. It has come to them all often before, so that there is nothing unfamiliar about it. He comprehends that life is continuous and that the loss of the physical body is nothing more than the casting aside of an outworn garment, which in no way changes the real man who is the wearer of the garment. He sees that death is simply a promotion from a life which is more than half physical to one which is wholly superior; so for himself he unfeignedly welcomes it, and even when it comes to those whom he loves, he recognizes at once the advantage for them, even though he cannot but feel a pang of regret that he should be temporarily separated from them.

Further study shows that even this supposed separation is in fact only apparent and not real, for he learns that the so-called dead are near him still, and that he has only to cast off for a time his physical body in sleep in order to stand side by side with them as before. He sees clearly that the world is one, and that the same Divine laws rule the whole of it, whether it be visible or invisible to physical sight. Consequently he has no feeling of nervousness or strangeness in passing from one part of it to another, and no sort of uncertainty as to what he will find on the other side of the veil. The whole of the unseen world is so clearly and fully mapped-out for him through the work of the Theosophical investigators that it is almost as well known to him as the physical life, and thus he is prepared to enter upon it without hesitation whenever it may be best for his evolution.

For full details of the various stages of this higher life we must refer our readers to the books specially devoted to this subject; it is sufficient here to say that the conditions into which the man passes are precisely those that he has made for himself. He who is intelligent and helpful, who understands the conditions of this non-physical existence, and takes the trouble to adapt himself to them and to make the most of them, finds open before him a splendid vista of opportunities both for acquiring fresh knowledge and for doing useful work. He discovers that life away from this dense body has a vividness and a brilliancy to which all earthly enjoyment is as nothing, and that through his clear knowledge and calm confidence the power of the endless life shines out upon all those around him. We have already said that what the uninstructed man usually calls his life is only one day in the real and wider life, and this brings us at once to the consideration of the great Theosophical doctrine of Reincarnation.

This is one which is very frequently misunderstood, and one of the most ordinary misconceptions in connection with it is to confound it with the theory of the transmigration of human souls into animal bodies. Suffice it to say that no such retrogression is within the limits of possibility. Though it is true that the physical form of man has evolved from a lower kingdom, when once a human soul has come into existence he can never again fall back into that lower kingdom of nature, whatever mistakes he may make or however he may fail to take advantage of his opportunities. Since this day of life is a day at school, if a man is idle in the school of life he may need to take the same lesson over and over again before he has really learned it, but still on the whole progress is steady even though it may often be slow.

Those who have not studied it, and therefore do not know all that it means, often feel great objection to this doctrine of rebirth. I have no space here to set forth the many unanswerable arguments in its favour, but they are fully set , forth in the second of our Theosophical Manuals by a far abler pen than mine. It should also be remembered that, like the rest of the teaching, this is not a hypothesis but a matter of direct knowledge for many of us.

Man gains very greatly, also, from obtaining an accurate idea of his place in the universe; his inherent self-conceit is wholesomely curbed by the realization of other and far grander evolutions, while at the same time he receives the very greatest encouragement from a definite certainty of the future that lies before him and the splendour of the goal which he will assuredly one day attain.

In what has already been written we have constantly had to take into consideration the existence of the third of our great truths, the mighty law of cause and effect, of action and reaction, or of the readjustment of equilibrium. If we wish to understand this great fundamental law, we must wholly dissever it from the old ecclesiastical idea of reward or chastisement, and we must apprehend that in nature the punishment fits the crime with absolute accuracy and perfection because it is in fact part of it, because the result which follows the cause is itself part of that cause, although it is the unseen side of it. Under the operation of this far-seeing law man is what he has made himself and his surrounding circumstances are those which he himself has provided.

Novel though this idea has been to many, it should not be difficult of comprehension. We are all familiar with the suggestion that as we sow so shall we reap; it is merely a slight extension of that thought to suppose that as we are now reaping, whether it be in circumstance or in disposition, so have we sown in the remote past of earlier lives. Indeed there is no other rational hypothesis by which the many inequalities which we see on all sides of us can be explained. For not only do surroundings and opportunities differ, but it is painfully obvious that men differ greatly in themselves and that some are in every conceivable way less evolved than others. It is impossible reasonably to account for this on any of the ordinary theories, without impugning the Divine justice, but if we once admit that souls are of different ages and therefore need different training we shall see that a flood of light is at once poured on the subject, and that its difficulties one by one disappear.

The gross and brutish man is simply a child-soul; where he stands now we ourselves stood once many ages ago; where we are now, there he will also stand after many more of these school-days which we call lives. And just as by looking back on the savage we may realize that which we were in the past, so by looking to the greatest and wisest of mankind may we realize what we shall be in the future. There have been and there yet are among men those who tower head and shoulders above their fellow-creatures in spiritual development; the Buddhas and the Christs, the great teachers and the philosophers — all these show us what one day we shall be, and so we see an unbroken chain of development, a ladder of perfection rising steadily before us, and yet with human beings upon every step of it, so that we know that those steps are possible for us to climb; and it is just because of the unchangeableness of this great law of cause and effect that we are able to climb that ladder — because, since the law works always in the same way, we can depend upon it and we can use it, just as we use the laws of nature on the physical plane.

If physical laws were subject to capricious variation, it would be impossible for us to utilize them, since at any moment our machinery might fail us and we could have no certainty of any kind in connection with its work; but just because we can invariably rely upon the action of gravity or upon the expansion of a gas we feel reasonably certain in our employment of these natural forces. Just in the same way when we know with absolute assurance that the qualities which we possess now are the products of our own thought and desire in the past, we have also indubitable evidence that our thought and desire in the present must inevitably build for us new qualities in the future, and therefore that we can make ourselves precisely what we will.

Not immediately, for growth is slow and evil habits take long to eradicate; nevertheless, with utter certainty. When we see clearly that our present circumstances are the results of our actions in the past we see also at the same time that we can so arrange our actions in the present as to mould our circumstances in the future, and thus we see that the whole of that future is entirely in our hands, subject only to unexhausted effects of what we have already done in the past. For neither thought nor action necessarily produces all its effects immediately. Sometimes it may be many years or even many lives before the full results become apparent; yet never does the slightest of them fail of final fulfilment. As the poet Longfellow has said: —

Though the mills of God grind slowly, yet they grind exceeding small;

Though with patience stands He waiting, with exactness grinds He all.

From this great Law flow many things. If once one gains this idea of perfect justice, the troubles and sorrows of life take on quite a new aspect. In the case of the ordinary person quite a small trouble will often, because it is so close to him, loom up so large as to obscure the entire horizon for him, so that he is unable to see that the very sun is shining. Everything is altered for him; all life takes on a gloomy look, and he believes that he is the victim of some especial persecution, when all the time the trouble in reality may be a very small matter. Such an attitude is not in the least possible for the student of Theosophy, for his knowledge brings to him a sense of perspective, and shows him that if suffering comes to him it comes because he has deserved it, as a consequence of actions which he has committed, of words which he has spoken, of thoughts to which he has given harbor in previous days or perhaps in earlier lives; and thus the whole idea of injustice as connected with misery is absolutely removed for him.

He comprehends that all affliction is of the nature of the payment of a debt, and therefore when he has to meet the troubles of life he takes them and uses them as a lesson because he understands why they have come, and is in reality glad of the opportunity which they give him to pay off something of his obligations, even though they may cause him much sorrow in the paying. Again and in yet another way does he take them as an opportunity, for he sees that there is, as it were, another side to them if he meets them in the right way. Far too often the ordinary man makes the most of his troubles; he anticipates them with fear, he intensifies them by grumbling, and he looks back upon them with regret and indignation.

The wise man spends no time in bearing prospective burdens, for he knows that nine-tenths of those things which people fear never come to them, and that even the few fears which are realized are never so serious in fact as they appeared beforehand in fancy; and so when trouble comes to him he does not aggravate it by foolish repining, but sets himself to endure so much of it as is inevitable with patience and with fortitude. Not that he submits himself to it as a fatalist might, for he takes adverse circumstance always as an incentive to such self-development as may enable him to transcend it; and thus out of the result of long-past evil he brings forth the seed of future good. For in the very act of paying the outstanding debt he develops qualities of courage and resolution that will stand him in good stead through all the ages that are to come.

Though it is true, as we have already said, that the student of Theosophy should be distinguishable from the rest of the world by his perennial cheerfulness, his undaunted courage under difficulties, and his ready sympathy and helpfulness, yet he will be at the same time emphatically a man who takes life seriously, who realizes that there is much for every one to do in the world, that there is no time to waste. Since he knows with such utter certainty that he not only makes his own destiny but may also gravely affect that of others around him, he perceives how weighty a responsibility attends the use of this power. He knows, for example, that thoughts are things, and that it is very easily possible to do great harm or great good by their means. He knows that no man liveth to himself, for his every thought acts upon others as well; that the vibrations which he sends forth from his mind and from his emotional nature are reproducing themselves in the minds and the emotional natures of other men, and so that he is a source either of mental health or of mental ill to all with whom he comes in contact.

This at once imposes upon him a far higher code of social ethics than that which is known to the outer world, for he discovers that it is demanded of him to control not only his acts and his words but also his thoughts, since they may produce effects more serious and more far-reaching than their expression on the physical plane. For example, one of the commonest vices in this age of overwork and overstrain is irritability. Very many people are suffering from this, and many are aware of the failing and are struggling against it. Every time that a man yields himself to this feeling and gives way to an outburst of anger, he habituates himself to the vibrations which express this feeling, and so makes it a little easier to repeat them next time and a little harder to resist the next force from without which may impel him in that direction.

But he also radiates these vibrations all around him and they impinge upon the emotional natures of other men and tend, like all other vibrations, to reproduce themselves. So that if some of those others be striving against this vice of irritability, his vibrations will stir them towards that emotion, and so make the task of control more difficult; and in this way by his own carelessness he adds to the burden which his brother has to bear. If on the other hand he makes a heroic effort and controls his own emotion, he sends out a vibration of serenity, of peace, and of harmony, which also tends to reproduce itself among his fellow-men, and makes it easier for every one of them to control himself in turn. Thus, even when a man is not in the least thinking of others, he inevitably affects them for good or for evil.

But in addition to this unconscious action of his thought upon others he may also employ it consciously for good; currents may be set in motion which will carry mental help and comfort to many a suffering friend, and in this way a whole new world of usefulness opens before the student. In this case, as in every other, knowledge is power and those who understand the law can use the law. Knowing what effects upon themselves and others will be produced by certain thoughts they can deliberately arrange that the results shall be good and not evil, for all who can think can help others, and all who can help others ought to help. Thus not only from selfish but from the far higher unselfish reasons the student sees the necessity for gaining perfect control of the various parts of his nature, because only in that way can he progress and only in that way can he be thoroughly fitted to help others when the opportunity comes to him.

Thus he will range himself ever on the side of the higher rather than the lower thought, the nobler rather than the baser; his toleration will be perfect because he sees the good in all. He will deliberately take the optimistic rather than the pessimistic view of everything, the hopeful rather than the cynical, because he knows that to be fundamentally the true view, the evil in everything being, as we have said before, necessarily the impermanent part, since in the end only the good can endure. In this way by looking ever for the good in everything; that he may endeavour to strengthen it, by striving always to help and never to hinder, he will become ever of greater use to his fellow-men end thus will become in his small way a co- worker with the splendid stream of evolution.

From what has already been written it will be seen that Theosophy is in no way unpractical or indefinite, but that on the contrary it has information to give which is of the greatest value to every human being, whether it be to the child or the parent, to the man of business or the artist, to the scientist, the poet, or the philosopher. Wherever it has spread its uplifting force has been felt, and already it has done much noble work towards the realization of the idea of Universal Brotherhood.

An examination of its principles will at once show that if they were generally accepted war between nation and nation or strife between class and class would become a ridiculous impossibility, and that its thorough comprehension could not but raise man's actions and thoughts to a plane far higher than at present. For this knowledge means not only power, but progress and unfoldment, and the spreading of the truth means the advancement of the world; and even if we take only the few leading points which have been mentioned in this little treatise we shall see that that must be so.

Surely all mankind would be better for the development of that serenity and joyousness which comes from the knowledge that all things are working together for good; for the entire absence of fear and worry; for the attainment of that wider outlook which shows us that no man can ever gain at the cost of another; for the widest tolerance and the deepest sympathy; for the attitude of universal helpfulness, towards the lower kingdoms as well as towards men; for the possession of a criterion by which all actions and all thoughts may be tried; for the knowledge that man is a soul and not a body, and that therefore the life of the soul is his life, and that his work here is its development; that death is something not to be feared but to be understood; that there is no injustice in the world, since people are what they have made themselves in previous lives, and have what they have deserved to have; that therefore they are absolutely the makers of their own destiny, and that every word or thought or action is a stone in that edifice of the future; hence that they are responsible for their thoughts, and it is their duty to purify and to enrich them, not only in order that they may themselves approach perfection, but also that they may be more useful to their fellow-men.

Those who will study this Theosophical teaching will find, as we have found who are older students, that year after year it will grow more interesting and more fascinating, giving them more and more satisfaction for their reason as well as more perfect fulfilment and realization of their higher aspirations. Those who examine it will never regret it; through all their future lives they will find reason to be thankful that they undertook the study of the magnificent and all-embracing Wisdom-Religion which in these modern days we call Theosophy.

THE WORK OF THE THEOSOPHISTS

I thank you for your very hearty welcome, and I beg to offer you my hearty good wishes in return. Bombay is, as you say, the gateway of India towards the West, and so it happens that those from Western nations who come here to learn often enter by it. But I would have you remember that, though the Founders of the Theosophical Society are both of Western descent, Those who inspired them and sent them forth to do that vast and wondrous work were not Westerns but Easterns — not English nor Russian nor American, but Indian. The Society was founded in New York, but the knowledge upon which it was founded came from India; and we of the West can never forget that.

You who were born in this country cannot possibly understand what a revelation Oriental philosophy was to us in Europe. You have all your lives been aware of certain great facts of Nature; you have known of Evolution, of Reincarnation, of Karma, and so you have been able to form a rational theory of life. But we in the West knew none of these things; a few advanced thinkers were working at the idea of the evolution of form, but had no conception of the evolution of the ego, or soul. We had to keep our science and our religion in watertight compartments; for the one studied the facts of Nature and the other ignored or denied them.
But here suddenly burst out a great light in the darkness, here was a system set before us which was actually credible and reasonable, which brought order into all the chaos and confusion, solved a vast number of previously inexplicable problems, and gave us not only a hope but a certainty of future progress. You cannot wonder at our enthusiasm.

You spoke of me as a pillar of the Theosophical Society, which rather amused me, for I certainly never considered myself from that point of view. I have always avoided taking any office in the Society, except that I was its Recording Secretary for the year 1885, succeeding in that office Damodar Keshub Mavalankar, the son of the first President of your Blavatsky Lodge. You mentioned some books that I have written, and spoke of me as an Occultist, a title such as that is far too great an honor for me; I have always thought of myself as a student to whom certain advantages have been given, in order that I might thereby render a little help to my fellow-students. You are of course aware that in some of the books which you mentioned I have only a small part, for in several of them I had the very high honour of collaborating with our great President. It is very kind of you to say all these nice things about your visitors, and I suppose that the best acknowledgment that we can make is to try to live up to the excellent character that you give us.

Having thanked you for your welcome, let me now turn to the serious business of the meeting. The Blavatsky Lodge, founded by H. P. B. and Colonel Olcott, was the first in India, and I think that I may very heartily congratulate you on its fifty years of solid work for the Cause, on the ability of many of its prominent members, and on the ready generosity which it has always displayed in connection with all Theosophical work. Now I have the honour and the pleasure of congratulating you on another forward step — the foundation of the Bombay Theosophical Federation.

I take it that the object of a Federation of Theosophical Lodges is always to bring those Lodges into closer connection with one another, and to establish a centre where all those members may meet at such times as they find convenient. You have in India two great Centres — the International Headquarters at Adyar, which is the true centre of the whole Society, and the centre of your Indian Section at the City of Benares. But the distances in this country are vast, and it must inevitably happen that there are many members who cannot gather at either of these points when the National Convention is held. It is therefore undoubtedly a good thing in the interests of the work that local Federations should be formed, so that those who cannot attend the great Convention may, nevertheless, obtain somewhat similar advantages without needing to travel so far. It is, indeed, a very good thing that our members should meet as often as possible. I am sure that all of you who have attended one of the great Conventions must have been impressed with the strong feeling of Brotherhood on such occasions, and the joy of old friends meeting again after perhaps a prolonged separation. Of course, there is generally on such occasions much to be learned from lectures delivered by some of the older members, by those who have specialized along certain lines, or by those who have more time for study; yet I think that the promotion and intensification of that strong and joyous feeling of Brotherhood is perhaps the greatest benefit of all. The more often we meet, the better we shall understand one another, and that is one of the implied objects of our Society.

It may be that sometimes there has been a tendency to forget that great central idea. We have so splendid and so fascinating a system of philosophy that it is very natural that we should spend much of our time in studying it, discussing it, and lecturing about it; but we must not forget that the very object of its promulgation is to explain and to prove the great doctrine that all men are brothers. We are so interested in our studies that there is often a tendency to argue about them, and sometimes in such argument a member becomes unduly excited and tends a little to forget that very Brotherhood which is the basis of it all.

I do not know whether you realize that there was a time in the history of our Society when its members were liable to expulsion if it could be shown that they had spoken ill of a brother member; I am afraid that if that rule were enforced in the present day, our membership would be suddenly and rapidly reduced. Those of us who try to follow most closely the teaching and example of the great Masters of the Wisdom are gradually allowed the privilege of drawing into closer relation with Them. Such fortunate pupils are always extremely anxious to help more and more of their brethren to share the advantages which they enjoy, but naturally their success in such efforts depends upon the qualifications of the candidates. I think that you would be horrified if you knew how many of our brethren have missed the opportunity of gaining those advantages by this one sin of malicious gossip.

I know how terribly prevalent it is in the outside world; but that is no excuse for us, who are trying to study the inner and higher side of life as well as the merely physical. We know perfectly the harm that is done by evil speaking and misunderstanding; the more we can meet together, the more we shall develop real brotherly feeling which will make misunderstanding and slander alike impossible. So I am always very much in favour of any kind of social gathering at which our members can come to know each other more intimately and to appreciate one another more truly.

You may have heard a little story of Charles Lamb which illustrates this point rather well. It seems that he was one day speaking disparagingly of a certain man, and the friend with whom he was conversing said to him: "You seem to have formed a bad opinion of this person; I thought you hardly knew him". "Of course I don't know him", replied Lamb; "if I knew him, I should like him". I think that is true of more people than one might suppose. I hope that this Federation will have splendid success in whatever work it may attempt, and that in coming to know each other more intimately members may be encouraged to work even more strongly and enthusiastically together than they have done hitherto.

There is one point that it might be well to mention here. Be very careful that in your enthusiasm for this new Federation you do not neglect your personal duty to the Lodge to which you belong. Each Lodge is in itself a Center radiating good influence over its neighborhood; and the amount of that influence depends upon the regular attendance of its members at its meetings, and the energy and perseverance which they display in carrying on its work. Never think of what you can obtain from the Lodge, but of what you can give through the Lodge. The Lodge must be a unity in itself, though also an integral part of the larger unity of the Federation. A Lodge in which there is disunion, in which there are bickerings, jealousies, carping criticism and personal ill-feeling, will not be a source of strength to the Federation, but a weak and vulnerable point in it. There must be nothing of that sort here, if we are to reap the full benefit of today's work.

Much of your Address of Welcome seems to me to consist of a statement [I might almost say a complaint!] that the lectures and writings of our beloved Krishnaji [J.Krishnamurti] have upset the minds of many members, and shaken their faith in theosophical teaching, so that some have even left the Society in consequence. This is obviously not the time for the discussion of such matters, as they have nothing to do with the founding of the Federation; but I shall be glad to deal with them as fully as you wish at our Question Meetings. All I need say now is that if any man's comprehension of the great facts of Nature can be so easily shaken, then it ought to be shaken, for its foundations are evidently quite insecure.

The system which is called Theosophy is simply a statement of certain great and incontrovertible facts of Nature; nothing whatever that anyone can say or do will alter those facts, so it is foolish to deny them or fight against them; it is wiser to adapt ourselves to them. The only question upon which there can reasonably be any discussion or argument is how that adaptation can best be achieved and that is what each man must decide for himself. Once more let me remind you that the Theosophical Society exists to promote Brotherhood, and to help to remove all the barriers to mutual understanding which arise from the differences of race, creed, sex, caste and color. It encourages the study of Comparative Religion, in order to show that all religions are fundamentally the same in their requirements, and the study of the inner side of Nature, in order that we may thereby draw nearer to the Reality which lies behind this outer Maya, and order our lives accordingly. This is the fundamental object of our Society; and all that is done and said on its behalf is done and said with the view of promoting that object.

If people do not understand the Oriental system of philosophy upon which the whole idea of Brotherhood is based, it has to be explained to them; and even here in this country, where everyone is supposed already to know a great deal of that, it is often necessary to remind them of it, and to show how the inferences that can be drawn from the knowledge it gives may be applied in daily life. Obviously the only reason that any person can have for leaving such a Society is that he has ceased to accept the principle of Universal Brotherhood. If he has reached that stage, I fear that he would be of little use to the Society, nor would it be of much help to him until he had recovered that much of faith.

Remember that we do not join the Theosophical Society for the sake of any teaching that it can give us, for practically all that we have received has now been published openly to the world — except for certain directions as to meditation and other practices of Yoga, in which instruction can only be safely given under strict promises. We ask no one who applies for admission to the Society what his belief may be; that is his own affair. We ask him only whether he accepts this idea of Brotherhood and is willing to work for it. Any man is always at liberty to change his point of view: he may receive new light upon some subject, he may look upon a truth from a new angle and so see additional facets of it. That is unquestionably all to the good. Truth has many facets, and the more of them a man can see, the wider become his sympathy and tolerance. The more light we can have on any subject, the better, so that the man's conception of it may widen out. But no widening of his consciousness should ever be allowed to interfere with the work that he is doing to help his brethren. It is true that in the course of its cycle of evolution the world is just now passing through a trying period, not only of commercial but of spiritual depression; a period in which a spirit of great restlessness, unreasonableness and unbelief is abroad. There has never been a time when the enlightenment of the Ancient Wisdom has been more needed than now. But can you not see that this very condition of affairs is a test for us — a test for the firmness of our foundations, of the living reality of our convictions, of our power to persevere under difficulties ? Are we coming well through that test, or are we not ?

There are weak brethren who say: "How can I know whether I am passing the test ? I am confused; I am uncertain; some teachers give this advice, others give that; I know not what to believe". Our Masters will not ask you what you believe; that, as I have said, is your own affair; but They will ask you what good work you are doing. You can know; you have an infallible criterion, if you will only be absolutely honest with yourselves. Are you living a higher, purer, nobler, and above all a more unselfish and useful life than you were ? Are you thinking ever less and less of yourself and your progress, less and less of gratifying your desires and your emotions, and ever more and more of serving your fellow-men ? Are you working more strenuously than ever ? If so, then you are passing your test; you are advancing, and our Masters' blessing will rest upon you. But those who for fancied self-realization or self-development forsake the helping of their brethren are moving backwards, not forwards. Deeds, not words alone, are the sign of real progress.

I have said that we do not join the Theosophical Society because of anything that we hope to obtain from it; we join it because we know that it exists for a good purpose — the promotion of Brotherhood — and we wish to take part in that good work. It is not for ourselves or for any benefit that we hope to gain that we band ourselves together in this work; for the work is entirely altruistic and is intended solely for the benefit of our fellow-men.

All work for the betterment of mankind is the Masters' work. Special lines have been indicated to us, and. we are doing our best along those lines; but we most fully recognize that there are many other ways of doing good, and we are always glad that our brothers should help to promote any of them. To feed the bodies of the poor is indeed a good and worthy act, and often it is all that can be done for them; to feed their souls with spiritual knowledge, if you are able to give it, is a still higher deed; but there is no reason why both lines should not be followed simultaneously.

Anything that can be done to promote or to help towards a sane, humane and rational education is good work — exceedingly good work; and I am very glad to hear that much has been done in that direction here in Bombay. Another splendid enterprise which our lady members especially can take in hand is the attempt to ameliorate the lot of women, to raise their standards of life, and to spiritualize the entire conception of marriage. There is plenty of good work to be done in the world, and every member of the Theosophical Society should be ready and willing to give help in any direction that he can. In this connection I should like to draw your attention to a very helpful list of minor activities which our good brother P. Pavri has published in his book on The World-Teacher.

At this present time it seems to me there is another undertaking to which every Indian Theosophist should set his hand if he has any opportunity of doing so. You of course understand that the Theosophical Society takes no part whatever in politics, and in that matter every one of its members is absolutely free to go his own way and to express his own individual convictions. But there is at least one thing in which we can all join, and that is the endeavor to promote peace and unity among Indians, to allay prejudices and to persuade all that Brotherhood is greater than sectarianism. The great Spiritual Hierarchy is striving to unify India, and it is precisely this lack of brotherly feeling which is the chief obstacle in the way of the achievement of that most desirable end. Therefore, anything whatever that we can do to help our brethren, both Hindu and Muhammadan, to rise above communal differences and realize that both are equally part of the great Indian Nation of the future, is obviously a direct piece of work on behalf of our Masters.

In some places there is a similar prejudice existing between Brahman and non-Brahman, and the same suggestion would apply there. No one need be asked, or should be asked, to give up his individual opinions; but once more there is no sense in denying the facts of the case — there is a difference between the presentation of religion by the Muhammadan and the Hindu; there is often a difference between the education and the outlook of the Brahman and the non-Brahman. But it is our duty to emphasize that, though these differences of opinion and outlook do exist, they must never be allowed to interfere with the far greater fact that we are all brethren, and must all stand together to make that Brotherhood effective. All Indians must learn to lay aside the purely selfish and personal point of view, and to look forward to and prepare for the magnificent future of this great country, of which all of them alike are children. We must think of that glorious future, and we must work for it; and the first thing to do is to bring these divergent elements together into one mighty force. If India is to be, as she undoubtedly ought to be, the spiritual leader of the world — if she is to fill her appointed place as the land through which the mighty forces of Shamballa may be distributed to the world, she must first of all overcome these petty rivalries and divisions which weaken her so terribly. Therefore we must all strive with all the energy at our command to promote unity, not asking any person to give up his private beliefs, but asking them all to join together for the purpose of this highest and noblest work.

Many other questions suggest themselves in connection with this. The opposition of all good men and women to child-marriage, for example, is based upon the scientific certainty that finer and stronger bodies are produced when both parties to the marriage are fully matured; and remember that such bodies as those are absolutely necessary for the great Indians who will take incarnation among us in the near future, and this present generation should already be providing such vehicles. I know that pandits can quote texts from the alleged Laws of Manu in support of infant marriage; but I think you should remember, in the first place, that you have absolutely no definite evidence that our Lord Vaivasvata Manu is responsible for those laws in the form in which they at present appear; and in the second place, that humanity is after all evolving, and that conditions have changed enormously during the thousands of years which have passed since the time when those laws are supposed to have been laid down.

Many of us have in the course of our work had the wonderful privilege of meeting the Lord Vaivasvata and serving Him in various ways; and I can tell you that He is an eminently sensible and practical person, and that His one desire for His Motherland of India is that she should progress in all ways, both physical and spiritual; and He will consequently be in favor of any movement which tends in that direction. We must unite, and we must remove from the Indian escutcheon these blots which disgrace its unique civilization in the eyes of the world. Our great President, who is especially His agent, has frequently written and spoken of these points, and her books and lectures deal with them far more satisfactorily than I can.

You have the admirable Organization of the Boy Scouts, in which each member is expected to do one good turn every day. A member of the Theosophical Society should go very much further than that; he should do many good turns every day, as many as he can; and he should ever be watchful for an opportunity to offer service. The Theosophist should be known to his friends and neighbors as one who is always ready to give any assistance or advice that he can, as one who thinks little of himself and much of the helping of his fellows. I trust that everyone of us may obtain that high reputation, and be careful always to live up to it; and I hope and believe that the work of this Federation will presently bring its members to that noble and desirable consummation.

I cannot end my address more fittingly than by reading to you a fragment which was found only a few days ago among

Madame Blavatsky's papers — apparently the conclusion of an article, though the rest of it is missing. It runs as follows :

> One eternal Truth, and one infinite changeless Spirit of Love, Truth and Wisdom in the Universe, as one Light for all, in which we live and move and have our Being . . . We are all Brothers. Let us then love, help and mutually defend each other against any spirit of untruth or deception "without distinction of race, creed or color".

Since this fragment has thus unexpectedly been discovered just before I left Adyar to come here, let us take it as a message from our noble Founder to our newly-formed Federation. Let us live in the light of this high ideal which she sets before us; let us steadfastly obey this command which she lays upon us, that, following in her footsteps, we may one day stand where she stands, that we may one day come to help the world as she has helped it.

www.ingramcontent.com/pod-product-compliance
Lightning Source LLC
LaVergne TN
LVHW041501070426
835507LV00009B/747